For You

By Reeona Barooah

Content

From My Heart and My Mind

Every time I hold your gaze,
I am in awe of your existence.
To see yourself,
the way I see you,
like the most perfect imperfect ever.

To see yourself
the way I see you.
You will realise how captivating you are.
You will realise how pleasing you are to my sore eyes.

Only if you see yourself,
by my eyes.
You will fall in love with yourself all over again,
Just like I did.

To see yourself,
the way I see you,
you will be amazed.
Just like I was.

My mind is so filled with you,
I can barely think about myself.
I wouldn't call my heart mine,
when it belongs to you.
It does belong to you even if it shouldn't.
Even if it's wrong.

If my heart can't have you,
then it won't take anyone else.
It won't ever accept anyone,
anyone but you.
All of me,
all for you.
'Why?' my brain questions often,
but the foolish heart of mine doesn't know why

-Will I ever know why my weak heart is truly and entirely
yours?

All the blisters that made me bleed,
are the ones he's healing.
All my scars you tried to hide,
are the ones he's in love with.
All my sufferings are his,
and his are mine.
All my flaws you hated,
are the ones he's falling for.

3 years ago

I was absorbed by your embrace, your tenderness. We were so full of each other; I was there in your arms while we were gazing at the stars and the beautiful moon. As you looked at me and said "The moon is pretty, isn't it?" It sounded more like a statement than a question. Oh, my beloved, this is when I realised that I fell in love with you.

yours truly

'Mine.' you say while I look at you and nod
because that's all I can do.
Do nothing but nod,
because you left me so speechless.
Don't look at me with admiration
while I was used to eyes of those that couldn't be mine
None look at me as you do.
None hold me as you do.

Again?

'Who are you?' he questioned like it's the first time he met me
Figure it out' I flash my grin foolishly
'Why can't I figure it out?'
Neither can I, sweetheart.' and here we go again.

As I take out my guitar,
the same one you taught me with.
As I blow the dust away,
and tears dropping from the eyes,
the same ones you awed in.
As I take my guitar,
and play the song —our song.

I pleasantly smile while the tears are draining out
not because I grieve you,
I have already grieved you enough by now, have I not?
I have grieved your soul
and retrieved all our flowers.
The flowers that now are wilting,
wilting on your graveyard,
while your body decays underneath.

-Maybe one day our souls will reunite.

My heart speaks

I want to know how it feels to love,
and to be in love.
I want to know how it feels to be loved
I can bear any suffering just to know
how it feels to be in love.
I would go through misery,
for us to be in love,
for me to love you
for me to feel loved,
by you and only you.

As our lips intervened,
I did naught but think of him.
Why him? I questioned myself.
How could I be yours,
if my mind is somewhere else?
Somewhere it does not belong.

What if I love again?
What if I fall in love again?
What if I start loving you again?
It will bring nothing but ache,
because I *love*, and you don't.
because I fall and you don't.
that will only hurt me and not you, will it not?

I listened to you play
I listened to you sing,
sing the songs we once loved.
The same songs that haunt me now,
haunt me with the memories of you,
haunt me with the ghost of you.
Oh, it's been years now,
how will I stop thinking about you,
when you keep coming back every year?

Loving you from a distance
seems like the only thing,
left for me to do.
I either despise you with all my heart,
or love you from a distance.
I would rather love you from a distance,
and look at you and her smiling at each other
like we used to,
than despise you with all my heart.

As it drizzled and you came running,
and swayed me around.
Who knew it would be the last time,
last time we danced
last time we gaze into each other
last time we laugh
last time I was ever happy.
Everything has a last,
and you were mine,
you *are* my last.

As he looks at me and asks;
What are you?
to me?

I pause in shock and say
whatever you want me to be

you flash your pleasant smile at me and question;
Would you call us friends?

I reply so quickly with a no
It sends a shiver through my whole body

as you took me in and never let go
I wish this would never end.
I wish *we* would never end.

-but everything comes to an end eventually

My eyes are drawn to her,
to her and her absurdness.
Her eyes are always high,
her hands are always filled with blood,
her own blood.
So bleak she looks.
She looks like there's no happiness left inside her

-this is what he described me as

You breathed life into my soul,
as our roots got connected,
as I started loving again,
as you gave life to my soul.
You took it away too,
the connected roots got rotten,
and you found another to bond with.

waves

as the wind hit the cool sea waves,
I was deeply focused on the waves,
the waves and its warmth consuming me whole.
The water absorbed me,
while I failed to notice the sand beneath it.
I was so consumed by the waves,
I failed to notice the sand consuming me whole
I was so in love, I failed to notice the bad.

-this is how you make me feel.

"You are not this" says he who I never opened my heart to.
What am I then? I question
and I look at him with disbelief,
as he vomits the words of truth out
and as he describes me.
He describes me in every possible way.
This is when I get scared,
scared of how he could read me
scared of how he could look into me; the real me

-was it something I said? he questions

Do you let yourself love, my dear?

Do you let yourself live, my dear?
The confined walls of loneliness.
The proximity of the self to the self.
The forced intimacy for oneself.

One day, the confined walls of yours breaks,
The proximity of mine is now yours,
Your scared intimacy and my indefinite love,
Do you let yourself love now?
If not, then let me love instead.
Let me love on your behalf as well.

Do you let yourself live now?
Live fully with me, my love.
Swim in the endless love for oneself.
The truth is, my loneliness collides with yours.

My anxiety dies within you.
My intimacy lies within you.
My fears subside within you,
In your love, my soul restarts.

Do you let yourself dream, my love?
In the darkness where shadows play,
In the silence where echoes stay,
Do you hear the whispers of the night?

Do you let yourself feel, my love?
If not then let me feel for you
Let me feel the emotion you suppress.
I would feel enough for the both of us nonetheless.

Despite everyone, why is it so,
that I only crave you?
Despite everyone in this room,
why is it so,
that I only want to be with you?
Why is it so that you have affected every breath of mine?
Despite everyone here,
I only want your embrace and no one else's.
Despite everything that has happened in the last years,
what is it so,
that pulls me towards you each and every time?

Platonic, is it?

*Friend — a very platonic as well as pure relationship between two
humankinds*

I would label our feelings as platonic,
label ourselves as *friends,*
friends who love dearly,

then why don't we feel like friends even if we describe ourselves
as friends?
Why do I feel more?
Feel something, I shouldn't
Something absurd and captivating at the same time.

- I don't think I am supposed to feel this

Same person, same feeling
oh love, what is it that we are getting out of this?
oh love, what is it that you want from me now?
Is it a piece of me that you crave,
or is it our old memories that you are bringing to light?
Is it comfort or is it love?
how can I be yours again,
if I can't be myself again?
oh love, how do I love again?

-I want to love again

Still the same?

I really wonder what would have happened
what would have happened with us,
if I didn't mess things up
will it be any different,
or will it be the same?
will we be the same,
oh boy, why do I realise it now?
Why didn't I think of it a year ago?

we could have been better
I want us to be better,
better for each other in fact.

-I am sorry for causing you heartache

What's the point of looking pretty,
if you are not here to admire?
What's the point of even being here, if you aren't?
What's the point of buying gifts,
if you aren't here to claim them?
What's the point of looking at the sky,
if you aren't here to talk about it?
What's the point of loving the moon,
if you aren't here to gaze at it with me?

there's no point if you aren't here.
you bring purpose into my life
you attach yourself to every materialistic thing I own
Every *thing* reminds me of you.

Fire and Ice

Ice should always be separated from Fire,
Yet the flames of the Fire desire Ice.
But what will happen to the cold when it melts?
And what will happen to the flames when it dims?

In the end, they will collide.
Not for their own betterment
but for their hidden desires that are buried within them,
If love could bring Fire and Ice together,
then is it possible for us as well?

The warmth of the flames burns into me
While the cold melts into you
The excruciating burns on my skin
And every shiver you make.
It is pure agony, is it not?

-      *Is this how love is supposed to be?*

When I see a glimpse of your laugh in him,
I wonder how similar it is.
I wonder how it sounds alike.
His laugh is as sweet as yours was,

you were equally bitter.

The Constant of my life

I think of us as The Moon and The Star.
You — The Moon and I — The Star.
We never seem to be apart.
As The Moon rises and The Star takes up the space in the sky,
As The Moon revolves around another,
The Star moves around with him.

You— The Moon and I — The Star.
You with the celestial beings and I with the sky.
Despite being with another, we seemed tied together,
–not by force but by a thread of strange affection.
The empty sky seems to be filled with our laughter and our cries.

You and I are never seemed to be apart,
–even when obstacles were in our way
A strange alliance and yet a loyal companion.

Where You are, I am.
When You talk, I listen.
When You love, I smile upon the two.
Where You are, I am.

"Why?" The Moon questions one night
The Star happily answers, *"You let me share your space in this sky.'*
"I am in love with another and thus I cannot love you, my dear"
he says
'It is not love that I seek from you. It is friendship that I seek for, my dear.'
she says
Thus, the friendship of The Moon and The Star began.
—Thus, the friendship of You and I began.

The Significance of You and I

Ring that cannot come apart from me and your presence that does not leave in peace. You awe while the moon shines and I awe at the sight of the majestic you. You; what are you really? A fragment of my imagination or a soul that's destined to be with mine? What are you really? Are you my first love or are you not? I imagine being apart from you and my nightmares would start. I sleep deep because in sleep, I would get to see you, in my dreams I would see you, in my imagination, I would talk to you with no consequences.

What am I really? An obligation in your life or a necessity. Do you get a glimpse of me when you gaze up at the sky? An obligation and a liability or am I not? Am I more or am I less for you, my love? What am I really? In truth, I am on a stage playing the role of a lover which would eventually fade into obscurity. In truth, the part I play in my life, is of a lonely person who cannot be attached to another but here I am, unable to detach myself from you. In fact, what am I to you really?

— Mostly what are we then?

Every night at 9, I sit at our diner.
Every night we talk at 10.
Every night we gaze at the sky at 11.
Every night we hold each other's eyes at 12.

Every day I wait till it's 9.
Every day I have news to tell you.
Every day I wait for the sky to be dark.
Every day I wait for my eyes to meet yours.

Every night after 12, you fade into obscurity.
Every night after 1, I try to uncover your absence.
Every night after 2, I find you.
Every night after 3, I realise you were never alive.

–Every night at 4, the ghosts of you haunt me.

The Soul aches and The Heart frails.

Why do you pull me in?
Pull me into this absurdness
I don't want to be involved anymore,
involved in your absurdness.

You will be there living your life with colours,
while I will have to lock myself in my darkroom again.
You will sing and dance,
while I will have to silence my voice with teardrops.
You will be there drinking and smoking with joy,
while I will have to create those scars.
You will be there making a mess in your house,
while I will be here cleaning blood

-my own blood

As you hold my face to face you,
I could see your anger.
I could see your disappointment.
As I let you hold me,
you can see my eyes saying sorry.
sorry for your anger,
sorry for your disappointment in me.
To the old me who held me tight — *I am sorry,*
sorry I failed you,
sorry I let others walk over us again,
and yet again I crawl back into them,
to be walked over again.

-to my own self

Storm

When those forty flakes besiege my abode,
As they dig deep upon thee trenches,
A tottered patch of my sins lay untouched,
Slow yet fierce it seems to churn my heart,
I lay limp draped in sheer cold.

When those forty flakes invaded my space,
it invaded my insides, clutched onto the ribs,
While it ripped my insides gently,
It whispered words of affirmations,
Yet clawed his nails digged my throat.
Smiled upon me, crushed inside.
Tendered me with its words,
While scared me with its trenches.

PRETENCE

I see those red marks on her wrist,
"I fell off the stairs." she says.
As I nod and let her accept that I believed her.
Oh this girl, how much will she fall off the stairs?
Those marks on her wrist,
Those hands pulling the sleeves to cover it.
Cover it from the eyes,
the eyes that roam around those hands.
If she were to be a feeling,
self-conscious is what I would describe it
How much will she hurt herself?
Will she stop when she finally tears off the beautiful skin she ruins?
Then what will be left of her to hide if there's no her anymore?

I notice her while her eyes are red and hands turning red,
I see her laughing while pulling her sleeves.
I see her smiling while wearing bracelets that strangle her wrists.
I wish I could see her being herself.
I wish I could see her in peace.
Perhaps in another lifetime, I could see her happiness.
Perhaps one day she realises that she can find solace.
Perhaps one day she realises that she doesn't have to pretend.

-Perhaps one day she stops with her pretence.

The woman who isn't loved enough,
enough for them to stay.
The woman who feels unloved.
The woman who is pretty,
but not pretty enough to be loved,
pretty enough to be admired,
but not enough to stay with.
"The other woman" as they call her.
She agrees while mascara spreads down her face,
she neither wipes it nor stops it.

He called me pretty and my heart grew.
He called me pretty and my inside glowed.
He called me pretty and I looked into his eyes.
He called me pretty while his eyes were on her.
His eyes were drawn to her while he called me pretty.
I wish I was pretty enough to keep his eyes on me.

Yet I find myself thinking about you again.
I can do nothing but reminisce about the past; you.
As I stare at the sky and observe the lines between the stars.
All I could think about was how much you talked about them.
From talking about stars to hating each other.
Look how the tables have turned.
I can do nothing but think about you,
about how you were, how you are and how you will be; *without me.*

From the sweet introverted shy guy to the guy who called me names,
to the guy who raises his voice at any minor inconvenience.
Oh boy, I wonder what happened to you.
Was it me who made you like this,
or were you like this all along,
pretending to be someone else,
someone you didn't want me to know about.
Someone I truly despised.

I am tired of this,
tired of the endless cycle,
the cycle i want to escape,
the cycle you do not let me escape,
the one where you pull me in again and again.
But I am tired of this now.
Oh, who will escape this if not me?

-to my heart

As I look at you and awe in admiration,
while you vomit the words of lies at me.
The lies— so sweet I couldn't see the bitterness in them.
Words of affirmation you fed me with.
Who knew all of it would be a lie?
Telling me that I am special,
while you awed in her elegance.
Oh boy, were you a good liar,
Or was I too moronic?

I look at him from the back of the class.
I observe how he smiles when he talks to his friend.
I observe how that smile comprises bitterness in it.
So bitter I could taste it in my mouth.
So bitter I do not want to taste it again

I see how those eyes have exhaustion written all over it,
written like it isn't meant for anyone to read it.
They just cannot notice that,
cannot notice he's unhappy,
that something is bothering him.
Something I want to figure out.
but he won't let me.

He's scared that I am going to tear him apart and see the truth,
The truth he doesn't want to tell anyone.
The truth I want to know.
I would taste the bitterness again and again if I had to.

To your nonchalant head,
get yourself together.
How much will you hurt,
only to save yourself?
Save yourself from you.
Oh, how much will you hurt,
till you stop?
When will you stop running away from yourself?

-you are your own grim reaper

He adores you– they said
No one can love you as he does.
He only loves the world for you
I smile faintly and nod.
Oh, only if they knew,
I am everything he ever hated.
and he has become everything I have ever hated.

Yet hatred isn't what we feel for each other,
but some pieces of us do not fit.
Why will I change my jigsaw puzzle,
while he messes with his own?
Something between us pulls
As I sit here looking up at him
while he looks down at me and says
Why is it so that I can hate all but you?

—*"He only loves the world for you"*

What do we hold?
You are everything I have always hated,
Then why can't I despise you peacefully?
Looking at me with hatred and love at the same time,
Oh boy, I have never met anyone like you.
I am all you have ever disliked,
Then why look at me with admiration?

oh, what do we hold?
love or hate?
why look at me with eyes of love,
While you vomit the words of hatred towards me?

My love, what happened to you?
The boy who loved unconditionally.
The boy who loved easily.
My love, what changed?
Did they do this to you?
When did you become this?
The boy who silenced himself.
The boy who does not care anymore

—But I of all people know that you can never be this.

One-sided is what you described our friendship,
while I dedicated my whole to you,
while I dedicated each writing of mine to you,
and yet you think you are the one giving and not receiving?
Oh, only if you knew,
how much your presence has affected me,
and how much you were involved with me.

Do not say I didn't love you enough,
while I dedicate my whole to you.
Do not say you love me,
while you ran off when I needed you by my side.
Do not say I did not love you enough,
When I loved you so much that,
the thought of you running away scared me
My biggest fear was to lose you
because then who else will I write for?

Drowned

I sunk in that loud music,
and you kept approaching me.
And I kept running away,
because I loved being high so much.
I didn't want to face the consequences.
I drowned myself in that loud music,
because that's all that was left for me to do.
I kept running,
while you kept trying to catch me,
yet you could not.

The possibility of different versions of you is better than the reality of you.

I cannot seem to find a perfect word to describe you.
Should I call you a tremendous liar,
or should I call you my lesson?
Look at us now.
You, with the people we despised together,
and I, with myself because if it's not with you anymore,
then it's with no one else.
What should I call you?
A hypocrite or just gullible?
A tremendous liar or my lesson?

-Instead, I wish I could call you my beloved.

The same eyes that looked at him,
are the ones that hold those bitter tears.
"It is fine." she says to herself often.
She says it as if she's convincing herself,
She's used to it by now,
used to people disappointing her — especially men.
The same men that made her feel at home,
are the ones wrenching her soul.
The same men that gave her peace of mind,
are the ones making her whine.

-The endless cycle of disappointment

What will become of us now?
Are we going to pretend,
pretend that we never knew each other?
pretend that we were not the best of friends?
pretend that I never meant anything to you?
pretend that you never meant anything to me?

Oh, my beloved, you were the one.
The one who I gave my all to,
The one I loved unconditionally.
I can do anything,
but act like you do not mean the world to me.

Even after everything,
I can never bring myself to despise you,
I want to despise you,
Because that would make it easier for me.
but in my eyes, you can never be a bad person.
Perhaps that's the problem.

-I think I can never stop feeling for you.

What has become of us now?
You believed all the lies they fed you with,
You believed everything you were told.
What has become of us now?
You think of me as an evil who causes chaos.
You think of me as a girl who shatters everything,
but I was there when you saw right through me.

You knew me,
I am the one who would go to any level for the loved ones.
I am the one who loves unconditionally.
I am the one who loves loving others.

But, look at us now.
You think of me as a heinous poison
and I think of you as waves,
waves that are never constant

When you entered my world, I held you tightly.
I held your hand when my circle crowded you.
I held your hand throughout.
I held your hand even more tightly,
in fear of losing you in that same crowd of mine.
I kept you close to me,
in fear of you feeling out of place with the group of mine.
I never once lost sight of you when you were in my space.

When I entered your world, you couldn't even bait an eye toward me

-I still wonder why

Only if I could despise you,
I would have.
only if I could be detached from you,
I would have.
But why is it that I cannot hate you?

It looks easy for you.
It looks easy for you to act nonchalantly.
If you can, why can't I?
If you can despise me,
Why can't i?

Oh boy, have I not tried enough?
Oh boy, have I not loved enough?
What is it that makes it easier for you,
for you to be detached?

-I wonder where I went wrong

A year ago

You were a part of me whilst I was a part of you.
Who knew we would be so enthralled with one another?
Slowly, the night became ours,
while the days faded into obscurity.
The night belonged to just us,
while the days turned to oblivion.
Tranquility only existed while you were a part of my reality.

– Oh, how I wish the nights are ours again

To my person, my beloved

Oh, my beloved, how shall I prove my affection towards you?
Didn't I already devote my whole to you?
Don't you notice how you consume me entirely that it aches
when you leave?
It aches whole-heartedly when you, *my beloved*, stop being
involved.
My soul was wholly about you,
but you tried reaching out to the person who poisoned my
existence.

My foolishness did everything to make you feel enlightened but
you; my beloved, ran off to consume the evil.
Instead of absorbing me in your arms, you escaped.
Instead of comforting me with your pleasant voice,
you started to sing for that corrupted poison you once despised.

Oh my beloved, was I not enough for you?
I did put up a fight for you when you suffered from grief
but when I dealt with heartache,
instead of embracing me with your tenderness, you befriended a
fraud.
Oh, my beloved, you were truly my favourite person once.

It's strange how thoughts of you are the only things keeping me
sane.
Besides you, the thoughts in my mind slaughter me every day.
It is painful to not think about you,
It is painful because you are the only thing rational
My only relevance to this agony,
My world burns in flames while thoughts of you cool my mind.
It is surprising, is it not?
Because all I want to do is tear off every skin.
Because all I want from me is nothing but the ashes that are left
out of me.
I wish I were a gentle flower; Instead, I wilt and decay.

Another version of us.

I often find myself wondering, partly about you.
Mostly about us, only if we could restart.
Only if there was enough time to refine.
Only if there were enough space to breathe.
Your voice tore me apart whilst your words engraved me.
Only if you did not torment me with your discretion.
While I tore my eye one by one and you fed me with your insensibility,
The truth is; I would have called you, I would have made the effort you deserve.
Only if your words of aggression were less excruciating.
What were you really? is the one question I keep asking.
I wonder if one day I will find out the reason for your animosity.
Only if I could bring myself to pick up your calls,
But sadly, the terror inside me won't allow me to.
I thank the terror, I should not but yet I find myself in solace with my terror.
At the end of the day, I find solace in my solitude.

Maybe now, I can allow myself to swallow my terror.
Maybe now, You and I can have *another version of us.*
A version where the past does not interfere,
Where we consume each other and not let go.
I will promise myself to you when the time does not intrude
When the time is finally right for us to hold hands and not burn in the process.
It is merely impossible for me to breathe the air where your scent doesn't linger.
Maybe in the future there will be hope for us.
Maybe one day you will realise that *it's always been you.*
Maybe one day your torment will end,
because it kills me to live a life where you do not exist.
Maybe after years you will realise that you are my only exception.
You are my sin and my salvation, my solace and my torment, my life and my death.

The Disparities

Death

Death is inevitable.

Filled with uncertainty, horror and **relief**.

Relief from the agony, misery and torment of the soul.

An escapism is what the great **death** is.

The soul floats away; while the body burns.

"Why did you leave?" is what the body questions while it burns

"I had to." the soul smiles upon the burning body

What it meant was;

I had to leave to be beautiful again, to be nurtured again, to relief
you from the torture; that is life.

I had to because even if the body was breathing, the soul was wilting.
Even if the eyes were open, the heart stopped.

I had to because neither you nor I can defy the great death. I am
content and I shall be content for the fortune that will further fall
upon me for a new life.

Loathe me now but you will be at peace later. You will be content
soon.

The journey of our life has come to an end.

-For my grandfather, may he be at peace.

The Greatest Pain

The greatest misery; I have felt it, I have consumed it and I have
swallowed it.
Partly because I was the one who crafted it.
Partly because I was the one who made myself feel it,
I made myself consume the agony
And I forced myself to devour it.

The scars I write about are the ones I gift myself with.
It would not be possible for a mere being to torment me.
Because the greatest pain I have ever felt is the one I gifted to myself.
While I was wilting from inside, I shone from outside.
This is why one day I decided;
I decided to wilt entirely and truly

The beautiful nails I nourished eventually dig deep into my skin,
The intellectual mind of mine has thoughts that bleed out of my head.
The caged heart of mine has stopped pounding for another.
My hands tremble as I cut a piece of myself and set it aside.
My eyes, sore as they bleed from the pain; the pain I made myself feel.
And my chapped lips longing for another touch.

Desperation

Please come back home, my dear.
Blame me, Accuse me, Yell at me.
Scream till your throat goes numb.
But please, my love, come back home.
Please do not treat me with your silence
Please do not torment me like this, love.
This excruciation is unbearable.

Please come home, my love
Be angry at me,
Love me not,
Forgive me not,
But, my dear, it is killing me to live without you.
This is torturous, my dear.
Do not let me live in this torment, my love.

Please come back home, my dear
It is not a home without your existence.
Please scream at me, my dear love.
Do not let me live in your silence.
Please let out your harsh words,
As it will give me a reason to hear your voice.
Accuse me with your fiery eyes,
As it will give me a reason to look at your eyes.

Please come back home, my dear love.
Death is neither exhilarating for you nor for me.
Please do not let me mourn you, my dear.
Instead, let me believe for the rest of my life, that you are living.
Let me believe that you are coming back home one day.
My love, did you not torment me enough?

Please come home and relieve me from this agony that is your death,
my dearest love.

"I am made of memories." he says

I, too, am made of something of everything.
I wonder at times, *what will be left of me if I stop writing?*
Words that could not be expressed out loud
Yet, it could be written so beautifully.

I, too, am made of emotions.
I feel everything and I feel extremely.
Either I feel a lot or I feel none.
Days I feel naught horrifies me.
Days I feel all have left me with blisters.

"Am I too made of memories?" I ask, more to myself.
I write because they once wrote me a poem.
I read because they could not stop talking about books.
I listen because none did when I talked.
Memories are crafted by me but am I made out of it?

"My dear, I am in your memory" he says
'I am naught but a voice in your mind.
I am naught but a vision floating in front of you.
I am naught but made by your own memories.
Believe me not, if you may, my dear.'

"How could it be when you are in front of me?"
"My love, I am naught but lifeless"
He says as I stand before his graveyard.
"I am buried, my love. I cannot come back home."
He says while the flowers in my hand wilt.
"Please, my love, live a life without me."
He says while I dig a hole for myself
      Do not mourn me, love but please, live for yourself, instead.

The Lethal Warmth

It is strange, is it not, my dear?

How deeply I feel; extremely and in excess,

which is neither good for me nor for you.

Because my dear, I only feel in excess in your presence.

Because my dear, it not only blooms but also aches.

My weak emotions, my encaged heart and my enraged mind.

All in a disagreement. Why?

Because, my dear, how are we supposed to live together,

when your flames touches my frost,

when your fire dusk and my ice melts,

Then, my love, what will be left of us?

Do we not die when we come into contact?

Do we not perish away?

My encaged heart says I should hazard it all.

My enraged mind swears at me to be rational instead.

My weak emotions cannot handle our warmth.

I am only left at my own mercy.

Because, my love, it is forbidden to bloom for you,

Because, my love, it is forbidden to ache for you.

"Perhaps, in one lifetime or in one universe, we do reconcile." you say.

Why not this one?

"Perhaps, when we perish away, our bodies will finally collide."

Maybe, one day we will hazard it all, for once, for our love.

"My beloved, you are my misery, agony and my torment."

He says while he burns in flames

"My beloved, perhaps one day you will realise that I already hazarded all for you."

He says while his ashes leaves his body

"My beloved, I must compensate for my atrocity."

My beloved, do remember that my love for you is the greatest above all.

The Inevitable Final War

While you fought in the battlefield,
I, too, was fighting for patience.
I calmly argued with Dear Lord,
as you took out our ancient sword.
I keep the aid ready,
while I wait in the garden.

I see a man who is severely battered.
I see a man who took a bath with blood.
I see a man whose limbs are giving up.
Partly, I see a little boy who feared violence.
Partly, I see a little boy who feared the sight of blood.
But mostly I see you, my dearest love.

Tears filling my face and mixing with thy blood,
while I rinse off the blood from your torso.
"How do you know it is me?" you question
'How could I not, my dear? I would always recognise you,
I would recognise you if I were still blind,
I would recognise your flesh and blood with a mere touch,
I would recognise you by your smell,
I would still recognise you by your voice, if I were to be deaf.'

Your head lying on my lap while your torso drains from blood,
Blood that is indeed, not yours.
In your last breath you say:
"Oh, my beloved , the blood is not mine."
'Then whose is it?'
"It is the blood of the ones who disregarded you, my beloved."
My tears are now mixed with yours.
"Take it as a token of my love for you, my beloved."
'But your eyes once feared bloodshed'
"Yes, my beloved, but there is very little that I would not do for you."
Drinking in the poison while your corpse lies on me,
because to be dead with you is greater than to live without you, my love
"I started the war for you and ended it with you, my beloved."

Sin

My vision is blur, and my hands are numb,
I stand in the middle of this room,
My legs discourage me from standing.
My hands are wrapped around knives.
And my body feels lighter.

I see several bodies,
Maybe a thousand or a million.
All lying on the floor,
while their blood is painted on me.
All lying on the floor,
while I bathe in their blood.
All lying on the floor,
while I look at the mirror.

I see several bodies,
I cannot see their faces.
Once I do, I tremble.
Either I feel fear, or I feel proud.
I see many faces,
Partly are mine and mostly are of men.

The different versions of me lie on the floor.
The one who loved too much and the one who cared too much.
The one who gave all and the one who received none.
The one who had scars and the one who scarred herself
All versions of me are now dead.

I see several men,
The one who bruised his own wife,
The one who abused his own mother,
The one piano teacher who mistreated his own student,
The one who battered multiple.
All those obnoxious men lie on my floor
while their blood reeks from me.

This is indeed my only salvation.

Jet and Ivory

My fingers feel both numb and lively.
As I sit here on *my* chair,
I feel both fragile and sturdy.
Either the ghosts of you haunts me or soothes me.
I could feel my legs trembling while my heart's at peace.
My heart's either foolish or rational.

As I sit here on my chair,
The remembrance of you burns through me
The reminiscences of our past eases me.
The memories when I sat on this chair.
When you looked right through me,
When you looked down at me,
When you said that love is the greatest above all.

As I sit here on my chair and wonder,
How could we love?
Jet and Ivory could never belong.
Then did we too not belong?
Jet with no morals, while Ivory strikes in wisdom.
How could we love?
Were our differences an obstacle or were we?

As I sit here on your chair,
While our house burns in flames.
How could I live when the ghost of you burns through me?
How can I love again?
Because for me love is not the greatest.
For me, *you*, my love were the greatest above all.
For me, our differences were our dearest.

For me, I could not live a life where Jet and Ivory can never belong.

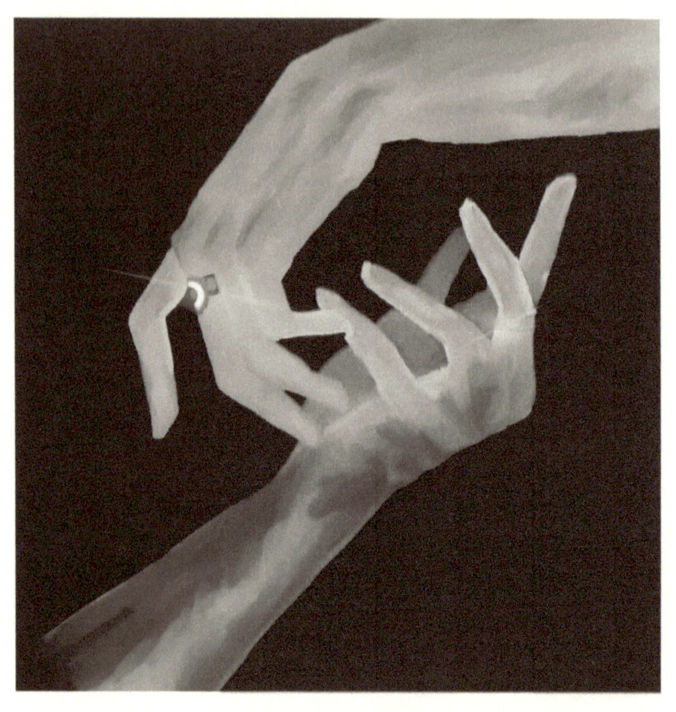

Your Ring and My Soul

Your ring and my soul,
        are tied together from body and whole.
Your ring and my soul,
        what was yours is now mine and what was mine is now yours
Your ring and my soul,
        I would rather burn in flames and keep what's yours safe.
Your ring and my soul,
        Am I really yours?

Your ring is not yours anymore,
Thus, it is mine entirely.
My soul is not mine anymore,
Thus, it is yours entirely.

Your soul and my ring,
        Are these justifications of our upspring?
Your soul and my ring,
        what was mine is yours, hence it can never be mine again.
Your soul and my ring,
        Are these a form of our endearment?

"Your finger is turning red, my dear." you say.
Let my finger turn red, I would not mind.
Let my finger bleed all my blood, I would not mind.
When your ring lies on my finger,
How could I ever mind?

            — Do we love or Do we not?

Do your words belong to you?

With space and time, I have realized your words are not your own.
The harsher your words are, the falser they are.
In truth, your mouth lies while your actions speak otherwise.
In truth, your words are not entirely your own.

You look me in the eye and tell me I cannot be loved.
You look me in the eye and tell me I do not deserve your efforts.
You look me in the eye and tell me I am intolerable.
Unlovable, undeserving and unworthy of your love, you say

If I cannot be loved, then why do your feelings fill the room with such intensity?
If I am undeserving, then why do you continue to give in to your best efforts?
If I am intolerable, then why do you stay by my side, enduring it all?
If I am all that you claim, then why do you still remain?

Your words do not harm me but in fact, it amazes me.
If I am as you claim, then why does your heart call my name?
If I am as unworthy as you say, then why does my pain afflict you, my love?
If I am as flawed as you claim, then why does your heart whisper otherwise?

In truth, your love is indefinite, is it not?
In truth, you hide yourself with your words, do you not?
I do not let your words torment me anymore, my love.
Do you know why?

Because I could feel the intensity of your feelings.
Because I could see your efforts that you seem to hide.
Because I could sense your pain, my love.
Because I could hear your heart speak instead.

– Your actions speak to me, my love, not your words.

I wish for many things

I wish for many things but mostly I wish you were here.
Do you hear the whispers of my heart?
Do you feel the desperation of mine?
Do you feel the intensity of my feelings?
Do you sense the proximity between us?

I wish for many things but mostly I wish you met my
expectations.
Deny me not as your eyes fought through the crowd.
Deceive me not as your hands tie the knot between us.
Forget me not as your presence fills up my void.
Hate me not as your lips speak otherwise.

I wish for many things but mostly I wish you were here.
Did you not care when I was at my worst?
Did you not get excited when I was at my best?
Did you not know how to express yourself?
Neither in my worst nor in my best were you there.

I wish for many things but mostly I wish you cared enough.
What will be the end of us — your ego or mine?
What will be the end of us — your people or mine?
What will be the end of us — your hatred or mine?
What will be the end of us — you or I?

— I wish you were still here with me

The Wild Love or The Right Love?

95

What do I seek for?
The wild one or the right one?
The former makes me feel it all.
The latter makes me feel like I belong.
What do I truly seek for?

Whilst the loud music, his hands hold mine.
Whilst the heavy crowd, his eyes find mine.
In this darkness, I can feel him.
In this eclipse, I can find him.
In this obscurity, I can sense his vulnerability.

Does the music that plays within me echo within you too?
Do you hear the whispers of my soul in this loud music?
You pulled me in once and I refuse to ever come back.
Will our contradictory world ever let us live?
At the end, will the same music that binds us be the reason we part?

Amidst the silence, he hears my voice.
Amidst the solitude, he feels my void.
In this transparency, his anger speaks to me.
In this clarity, his eyes blame me.
In this harmony, his soul is rooted to mine,

Does the void that lies within me rest within you too?
Do you hear my voice in this silence?
I wish I could come back to my world for you.
Will my sin collide with your salvation?
At the end, will we finally have another version of us?

How could I ever choose between the two?
One in the loud music and another in the silence.
One finds me in chaos and another hears me in silence
Do I ever choose between the two?
If I do, then who do I lose?

Was thy shunned or was thy forgotten?

Tell me, my dear. Were you scorned or were you abandoned?
Were you not precious enough to be remembered?
Was it your fault or was it theirs?
Tell me, my dear. Was thy shunned or was thy forgotten.

Amidst all, you were the only one left.
Amidst all, were you or were you not alive in the Grand Castle?
Born to be The Queen but yet abandoned by many.
Were you or were you not claimed to be treasured?

My dear, do you let yourself love?
Let me love instead.
Let me love you for you.
Let me love you on your behalf.

Amidst all, You and I are the only ones left.
Born to be loved by many but yet loved fully by me.
The forsaken forbidden love of mine.
I shall love for you and love on behalf of you.

If thy oughtn't love on your own behalf,
then how could your people ought to love you, my dear?
The animosity you carry for yourself would be the ruins of you.
Tell me, my dear. Was thy shunned or was thy forgotten

"I was neither shunned nor was I forgotten.
My animosity could not be the decline of my origin
My love could be defined as the destroyer
My love for only you would be the ruins of me."

My Deity

My Deity

My mother ceased on the day I was born. It was indeed a mourning day for all as it was the death of the dearest Queen of our nation.

'Fie! Fie! The Greatest Queen expired as a consequence of this child, that is a girl. A girl!'

'Neither a warrior nor a fighter but a girl!'

'A girl! A disgrace indeed!'

These were the only cries of all the commoners. Whilst everyone was disheartened by my birth, my father smiled upon me and said 'Such a beautiful creation and eyes like her mother.'

He looked at the ones present and said 'She is my daughter, my heir and thus your crown princess. Anyone who disregards her, disregards me. Henceforth, respect thy royal highness.'

Growing up, I was surrounded by many people but mostly I was raised by my father. The days my father was out in the battlefield horrified me and the days he was unarmed made me more cautious. The nights I dreamt the death of my father; the king were the worst nightmares.

It has been eighteen years since the death of my mother and everyday since I sit below the giant tree at the left bank of the stream that never seems to stop waving its waters at me. I find myself at this particular vicinity every evening since my eighteenth birthday whilst everyone takes a nap.

I smiled upon the water flowing nearby and on one particular evening a shadow appeared across the stream, I imagined it to be an animal but instead it was a man. *A man.* I could see his features across the stream, it seemed his hair was made from the mixture of the sun and the moon and his eyes were the colour of the beautiful Earth and the crystal clear water, the greatest shade of blue indeed. I wish his face was not as chiselled as it appears to be, he is indeed a unique creation of Dear Lord.

Every evening since, he always appeared on the right bank of the stream whilst I was on the left bank. Instead of smiling upon the water passing by, I admired him whilst he smiled. We have never said a word to one another. Neither did I know his name nor did he know mine. I wondered if he was a commoner or a traveller, perhaps a royal from another nation as he never failed to look regal.

Days pass by and every evening our eyes are hooked till the sun goes down and we disappear into the real world. My father never questioned what I do while I go away every evening but he did notice that I was content.

One evening he was immensely late and thoughts of him never coming back crossed my mind. 'Your eyes beshrew me.' a deep voice said and there he was. He swiftly sat beside me and I said 'How so?'

'They have cast a spell on me.'

'How so?' I questioned again

'I can neither contemplate on anything else nor can I stop thinking about your vibrant and fiery eyes.'

Ever since, our meetings are constant. One day a word goes around that the king is searching for a perfect suitor for me which is untrue. The following evening he comes by and firmly sits, taking my hand and says 'My love, let us run away together from this absurdness.'

I am puzzled by his approach and he continues 'Your father; the king would never grant me your hand in marriage. I am indeed the son of the king that is the archnemesis of your father. Our ancestors grew in hatred and so did our fathers and we too had to abide by that but my love, I can never feel the hatred that I am supposed to as a crown prince.'

'I can never resent you, my beloved' I say

'Then, run away with me, my love'

'I cannot.'

'Am I not dear to you?'

'Yes' I say 'Yes, you are very dear to me, my beloved'

'Is thy king dearer than I?' he questions with a taste of distaste

'Yes.' I say "The king; my father is dearer to me.'

'Why so?' He questions with animosity

'My father is the dearest to me. Anyone who crosses him has to pass through me first. Anyone who wants to fight him has to fight against me. My love and my devotion towards him is eternal. Henceforth, my love towards him is greater than my love for any other mankind.'

My Patience

How am I supposed to let go and move on when you have left an enormous amount of memories? Do you expect me to let go of you as easily as you did? Do not accuse me of not fighting for you. Do not accuse me of not loving you enough while it was you whom I loved unconditionally.

How am I supposed to forget you when you are everywhere? You leave behind every piece of yourself, every part of yourself. I cannot talk to a new person without seeing your resemblance in them. How was it so easy for you and so difficult for me? Maybe because in the end, I was the one who loved more. In the end, I fought, I loved and I got hurt.

I cannot call you my first *heartbreak* because my heart was never yours in the first place, but yet why does it feel worse than a heartbreak? I cannot call you my love because you were never mine to begin with. You were hers, so why did we act oblivious? I was never yours then why did you treat me like I was?

Why fight with her for me when you couldn't fight for us in the end? It was you whom I was looking at from that stage, it was you who I could see, who I could focus on in that room filled with hundreds of people. It was not my love whom I looked at first, it was you. It has been you for a very long time and you fail to realise it.

-I miss how we used to be

At the end of the day, I lay my head while wondering about you, I often tend to question myself about what would have happened if you were still here. I think of every conversation we would have had if you were with me laying your head beside me. Would you be angry? Would you be proud? Or, *would you still be in love?*

If you were still connected to my roots, would we feel more? I remember the days when a mere touch of yours would spark right through our bodies, do you ever wonder about the spark? Is it dead or does it still live inside us that we fail to acknowledge?

Do you reminisce about us as I do? Do you too lay your head and think about what could have happened if I were beside you? I was so consumed by your embrace that day that I felt nothing around me but your presence.

As I close my eyes and fall back to those days when nothing mattered but us, to those days when the night used to be ours and the day swallowed us with work. As I slowly fall asleep with a last question in my head; *"what if the night becomes ours again?"*

Acknowledgement

There are a lot of people who helped me make this book a reality, so this is my moment to say thank you to all of you.

To my family– Thank you Mom and Dad for always supporting me no matter what and helping me through the entire process of publishing this book and to my younger brother, Reyaansh who never stopped asking me all the meanings behind my writings.
I want to thank my entire family for always believing that I would do good in life and to my late grandfather, I hope you are proud of me and I wish you were here to celebrate all my achievements.
Lastly to Rivaan (Dhuun) — You have grown a lot and as your big sister, I am proud of how you have turned out. Thank you for taking care of the Barooah family dynamics and mostly me.

To my readers – Because of you, this book could be a reality and each of you reading my book means the world to me. Thank you from the bottom of my heart for your love and support. I hope you enjoyed *For You* because this book is dedicated to each and every one of you.

To Bhargabi and Urmi — The illustrators of this book, I do not know what I would have done without the both of you. The both of you helped me a lot in the making of this book and thank you for knowing what exact drawing I want for the book cover and the poems. Thank you Bhargabi for the numerous advice of yours and thank you Urmi for listening to me yap about the book.

To Mayank — To my constant, my supporter and whatnot. This gratitude is not solely for the guidance in the process of publishing this book but it is for everything you have done for me. You have been by my side regardless of the worst situations and thank you a lot for giving me lots of inspiration to write about.

To Utkarsh — Finally the person who got me into writing, if it weren't for you, I do not think I would be publishing my second book. Thank you for being my biggest supporter throughout everything and listening to each and every thing I could possibly talk about. Mostly, thank you for believing in me. I do not think these mere words could describe the role you play in my life.

To Emeline — No matter how many ups and downs we have, at the end of the day, we will always have each other. After every argument our friendship only becomes stronger and I hope you know that my love for you is indefinite and thank you a lot for giving me ideas to write about.

To Angel — It's strange how fast you have grown up, from running with other kids to talking so maturely, it's truly beautiful to see how you have become. Having you in my life is truly a blessing, thank you for understanding me like no other.

To Trisha – I truly believe that you would do good in life only if you let yourself shine. To 15 years of our friendship and more, thank you for being a better friend. Being with each other for over a decade is not a joke. You have been my best friends since we were children and I hope we grow old together no matter what

To Vairaaj and Ebhon— Life wouldn't be full without gossiping and ranting to the two of you.
To Vairaaj, Thank you for the forced princess treatment and all the affection you shower me with.
To Ebhon, my favourite gossip princess and my days would not be fun without you and your 'misbehavior'

To Abhimanyu, Aditi, Anisha, Aryaan, Atiksh, Palchin and Pranit — Thank you for being with me through thick and thin. You all never fail to laugh at my lame jokes. (even if it's obvious that you are laughing at me instead) Thank you for always making me smile and laugh.
To Shristi and Sreela --- My S Square, y'all never fail to brighten up my day. Two of the best people I met this year :)

Author's Note

Poetry has become a way to find solace with my own self. Every poem or writing holds a piece of myself with it. It has all my emotions that I find difficult to express. The poems in this book are created by my imagination and might be relatable to some people. It means no harm to anyone and this book consists mostly of poems and writings of various topics and no particular topic of any sort. I hope you enjoy reading this book!